James Carter

BY REBECCA RISSMAN

The Child's World®
childsworld.com

Published by The Child's World®
1980 Lookout Drive • Mankato, MN 56003-1705
800-599-READ • www.childsworld.com

ISBN 9781503816480
LCCN 2016945616

Printed in the United States of America
PA02322

ABOUT THE AUTHOR

Rebecca Rissman is a nonfiction author and editor. She has written more than 200 books about history, science, and art. She lives in Chicago, Illinois, with her husband and two daughters. She enjoys hiking, yoga, and cooking.

Table of Contents

★ ★ ★

Jimmy Carter was nothing but smiles with the leaders of Egypt and Israel on March 26, 1979.

CHAPTER ONE

Carter Makes Peace

★ ★ ★

It was March 26, 1979. The president of Egypt stood outside the White House. The **prime minister** of Israel was there, too. The two leaders smiled. They shook hands. Photographers snapped photos. This was a **historic** moment. People clapped. President Jimmy Carter stood between the two leaders. He smiled. He placed his hands around theirs.

Egypt and Israel had been at war since 1948. The countries had many deadly fights. Carter worried about the anger between them.

The peace treaty that Egypt and Israel signed was also called the Camp David Accords.

He thought it was very unsafe. He worried their war could affect other people. Carter wanted to help Israel and Egypt find peace.

Carter invited the leaders to Camp David in Maryland. This was a peaceful place. Carter helped the visiting leaders talk about their problems. It was not easy. Both leaders were upset about many things.

Carter was successful after two weeks of work. Egypt and Israel made a peace treaty. This was an agreement that would end the war. The agreement stated that Israeli soldiers would leave Egypt. Egypt would also recognize Israel as a nation.

Carter worked hard to solve problems when he was president. He spent his time helping people around the world. Carter tried to help leaders from different countries agree. He wanted to stop wars. He wanted to keep people safe. Carter also helped people in the United States.

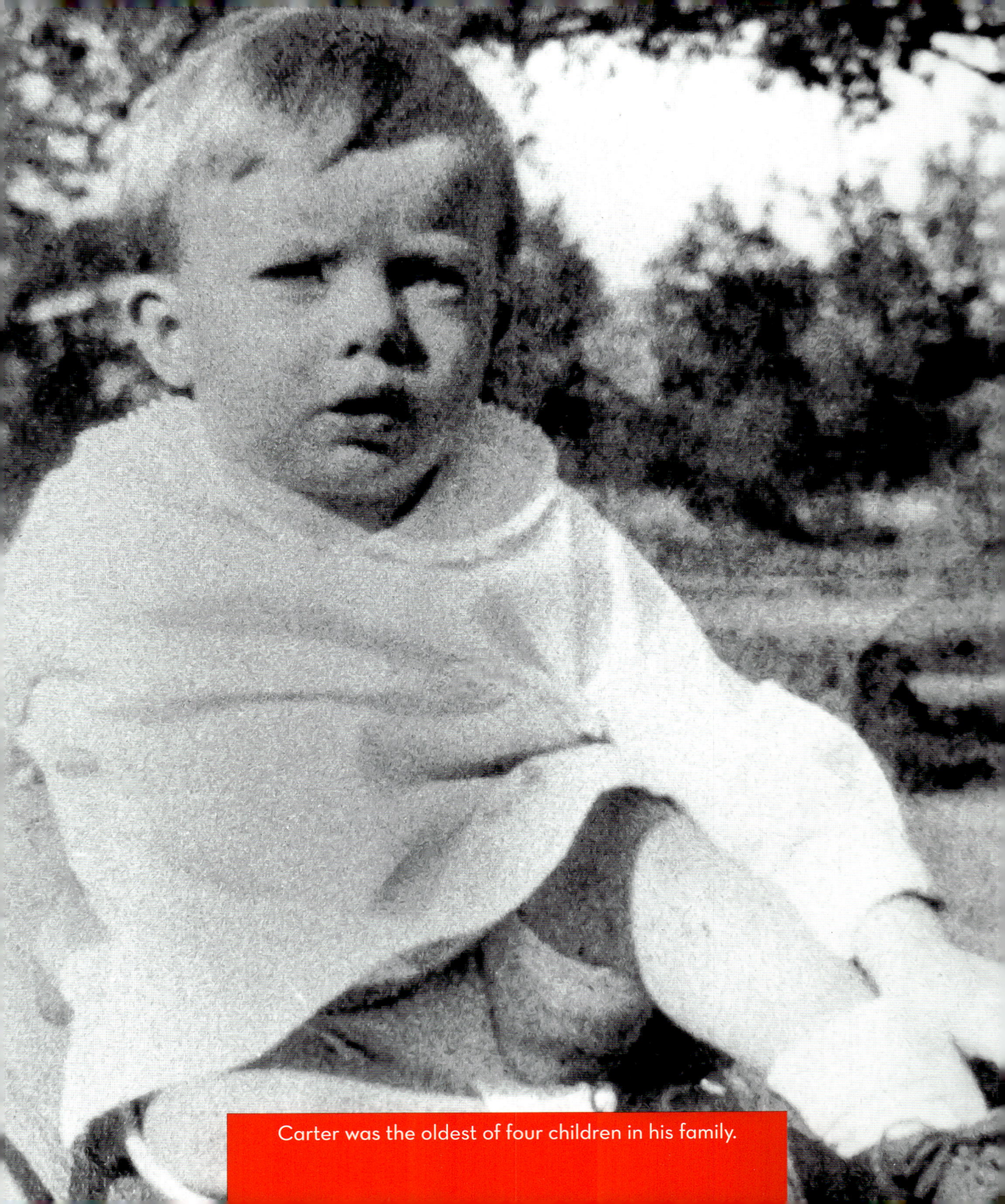

Carter was the oldest of four children in his family.

CHAPTER TWO

A Hardworking Boy

★ ★ ★

James Earl Carter Jr. was born on October 1, 1924. He was from Plains, Georgia. His family called him Jimmy. His mother was a nurse. His father was a farmer. His father also owned a store. Jimmy helped his father whenever he could.

Jimmy enjoyed learning. He studied often. He attended a **segregated** school. This meant it was only for white children. No African Americans were allowed to attend. Jimmy had many African American friends at home. He did not think they should be separated.

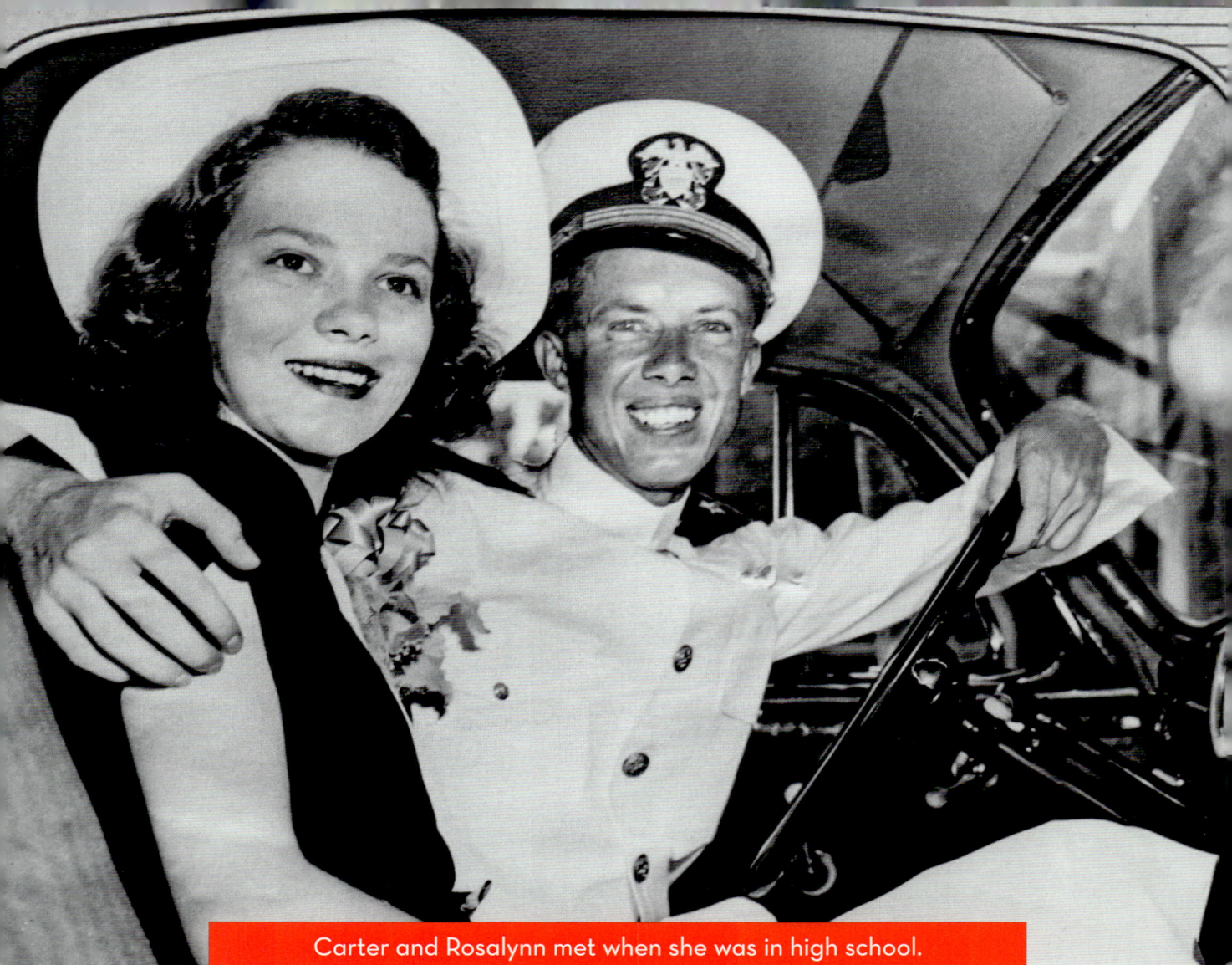

Carter and Rosalynn met when she was in high school.

Jimmy was a hard worker. He earned money working at his family's store. When he was 13 years old, he bought five small houses. People could rent them. This helped him earn more money.

Jimmy was interested in the U.S. Navy. He went to the U.S. Naval Academy. It was in Annapolis, Maryland. He was 19 years old. Jimmy did not fit in well at school. He was small and quiet. But he was a hard worker. He was at the top of his class.

Jimmy finished school. He married Rosalynn Smith in 1946. Then he became an officer in the navy. He worked on submarines. Jimmy and Rosalynn had three sons. They later had one daughter.

In 1953, Jimmy's father died. His father's businesses began to fail. Jimmy's mother needed help, too. So Jimmy moved his family back to Georgia. He took over his father's store and farm. Soon, they became successful again.

Civil rights supporters wanted to end school segregation.

CHAPTER THREE

"I'll Never Tell a Lie"

★ ★ ★

Carter did not fit in well in Georgia. Some people living there wanted segregation. Carter did not. He **supported** the **civil rights** movement. This was an effort to get rid of segregation. Some people in Georgia hated his ideas. They hung hurtful signs on his house. Carter thought they were wrong.

Carter became interested in **politics**. He thought Georgia needed someone new in office. At first he had trouble winning elections. His ideas about civil rights were unpopular. But he kept trying.

Finally, he succeeded. Carter was elected to Georgia's senate in 1962. He was reelected in 1964. Then he became governor of Georgia in 1970.

In office, he worked to help African Americans. He appeared on the cover of *Time* magazine in 1971. The magazine said he was a new type of politician. His ideas about race were different. He helped people change their minds about civil rights.

Carter decided to run for president. He ran against Gerald Ford in 1976. Carter told people "I'll never tell a lie." He wanted them to know he was honest.

Carter won the election. He worked hard to improve the **economy**. Oil cost a lot of money. Americans were spending more on it than ever. Carter created the Department of Energy. It helped lower oil prices. He also worked to find better energy sources.

Carter had many goals for himself as president. He wanted to help the environment. He turned land into National Parks. These parks protect wildlife.

Carter also wanted to help people of color. He wanted to help women, too. He gave many government jobs to women. He hired many non-white people.

Carter believed that peace around the world was important. He worked to end the Egypt–Israel war. He formed relationships with other countries, too. But Carter also had troubles overseas. In 1979 there was a big problem. Students in Iran took over the American **embassy**. The students were angry with the United States. They were mad that America helped Iran's past leader. The students took more than 50 Americans as **prisoners**. Carter asked Iranian leaders to let the Americans go. But they refused.

Many Americans thought Carter was a failure. They blamed him for the weak economy. Americans thought the prisoners were Carter's fault, too.

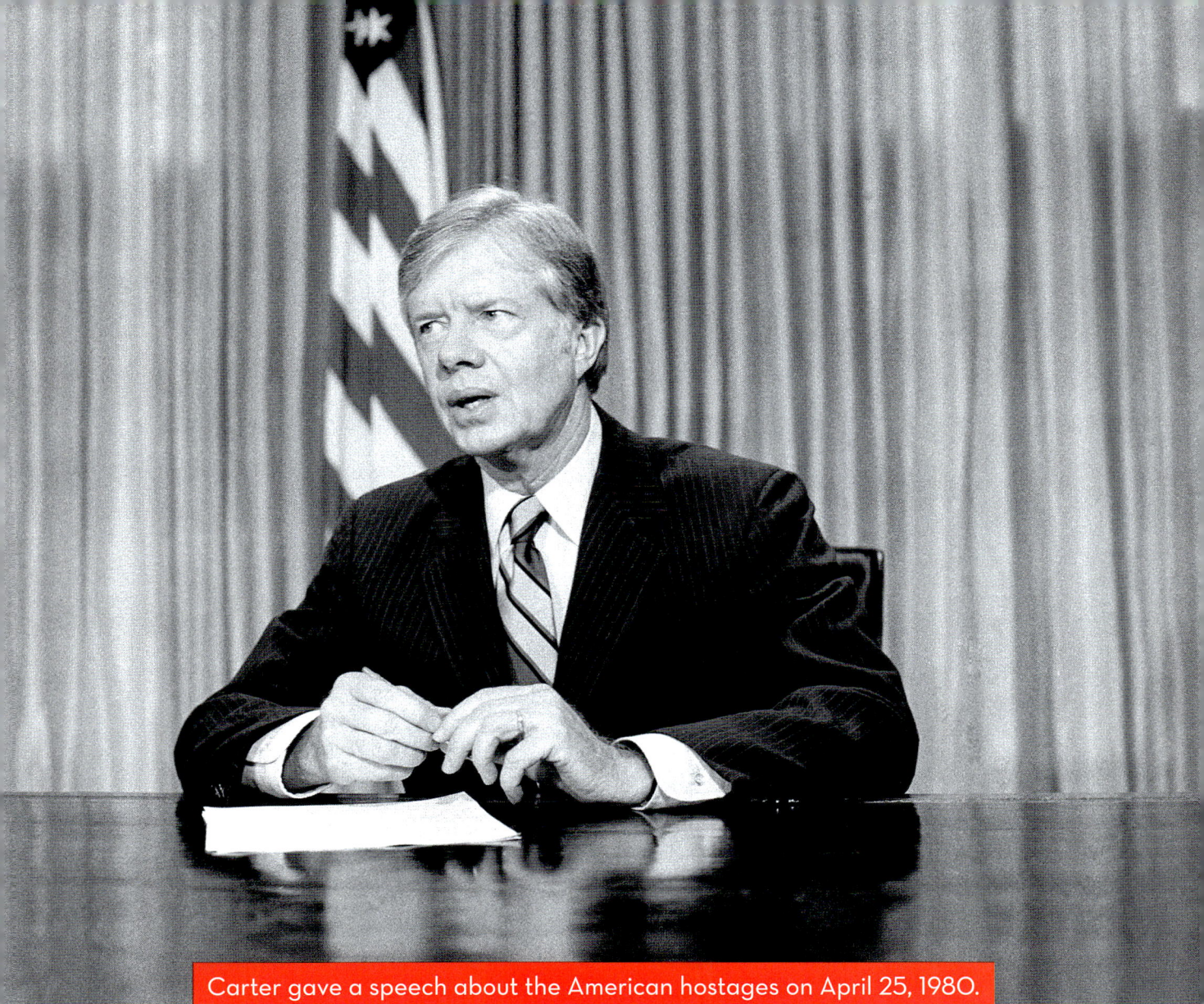

Carter gave a speech about the American hostages on April 25, 1980.

In 1980 Carter ran for president again. He lost to Ronald Reagan. The American prisoners were freed on January 20, 1981.

Carter has worked for dozens of causes,
including building houses in China.

CHAPTER FOUR

Continuing to Work for Peace

★ ★ ★

Carter left the White House. But he did not stop working. He started a **charity**. It is called the Carter Center. The center helps the poor. It looks for ways to heal illnesses. It also works to spread peace around the world.

Carter also spent time helping other governments. He traveled to different countries. He helped in their elections. Carter made sure the elections were fair.

Carter then became involved in education. He worked at Emory University in Atlanta, Georgia. He also wrote books. Some of his books are about politics. Others are about his life.

In 2002 Carter won a Nobel Peace Prize. This is a major award. It is given to people who help the world. The award was for Carter's charity work. It was also for his part in the Egypt–Israel agreement. Carter gave a speech. He said people should work together for peace.

In 2015 Carter became ill. He was treated and soon recovered.

Some people thought Carter was a good president. Others thought that he made mistakes. But many know him for his charity work. They remember how he helped people around the world.

Carter accepted his Nobel Peace Prize on December 10, 2002, in Norway.

TIMELINE

1920

← **October 1, 1924** James Earl Carter Jr. is born in Plains, Georgia.

← **1943–1946** Carter attends the U.S. Naval Academy in Annapolis, Maryland.

← **July 7, 1946** Carter marries Rosalynn Smith.

← **1953** Carter moves home to Georgia to help the family business.

← **November 3, 1970** Carter is elected governor of Georgia.

← **November 2, 1976** Carter is elected president.

← **March 26, 1979** The Egypt–Israel peace treaty is signed.

← **November 4, 1979** Americans are taken prisoner in Iran.

← **November 4, 1980** Carter loses the presidential election to Ronald Reagan.

← **October 11, 2002** Carter wins the Nobel Peace Prize.

← **August 12, 2015** Carter announces he is sick with cancer.

← **December 6, 2015** Carter announces his cancer has been successfully treated.

2015

GLOSSARY

charity (CHAYR-i-tee) A charity is an organization that helps people in need. Carter started his own charity called the Carter Center.

civil rights (SIV-il RITES) Civil rights are rights that everyone should have, regardless of their race, age, gender, or religion. Carter supported civil rights for African Americans.

economy (i-KON-uh-mee) The economy is a system through which goods and services are sold and bought. During Carter's presidency, the U.S. economy was in trouble.

embassy (EM-buh-see) An embassy is where an ambassador, someone who represents their government in another country, lives. Students took Americans hostage from the American embassy in Iran.

historic (hiss-TOR-ik) Historic means an important event in history. When Carter shook hands with the leaders from Iran and Egypt, it was a historic moment.

politics (POL-uh-tiks) Politics are activities to gain or hold onto power in government. Carter became interested in politics when he lived in Georgia.

prime minister (PRIME MIN-uh-stur) A prime minister is the head of government in certain countries. The prime minister of Israel met with Carter at the White House.

prisoners (PRIZ-uhn-urs) Prisoners are people who have been captured and kept against their will. While Carter was president, Americans were taken as prisoners in Iran.

segregated (SEG-ruh-gated) To be segregated means to be set apart or separated from other groups of people. Carter did not think African Americans should be segregated from white people.

In the Library

Haldy, Emma E. *Jimmy Carter*. Ann Arbor, MI:
Cherry Lake Publishing, 2016.

Hobkirk, Lori. *James Earl Carter*.
Mankato, MN: The Child's World, 2009.

Piven, Hanoch. *What Presidents Are Made Of*.
New York, NY: Atheneum Books, 2012.

On the Web

Visit our Web site for links about
James Carter: **childsworld.com/links**

*Note to Parents, Teachers, and Librarians: We routinely verify our Web links to make
sure they are safe and active sites. So encourage your readers to check them out!*

INDEX